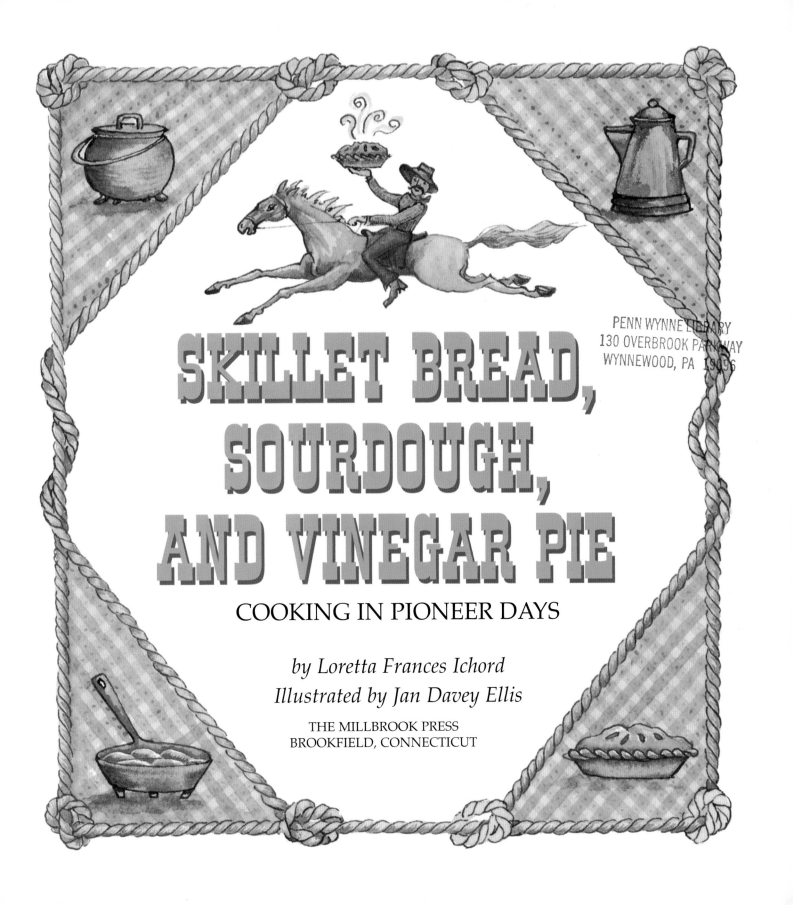

SKILLET BREAD, SOURDOUGH, AND VINEGAR PIE

COOKING IN PIONEER DAYS

by Loretta Frances Ichord

Illustrated by Jan Davey Ellis

THE MILLBROOK PRESS
BROOKFIELD, CONNECTICUT

*For my beloved father, Lloyd A. Duffey, who had
the heart of a pioneer.* LFI

*For my father, William Davey, whose pioneer spirit
has been an inspiration.* JDE

I would like to thank my editor, Jean E. Reynolds, for her enthusiasm,
kindness, and hard work. I am also grateful to all the friendly and knowledgeable
people, many descendants of pioneers, that I met in museums, forts, and historical
landmarks as I researched my way across the Oregon Trail. Finally, a special
thanks to Norman and Gaynelle Park, who let me view Devil's Gate at Dumbbell
Ranch, their scenic cattle ranch in Wyoming.

Library of Congress Cataloging-in-Publication Data
Ichord, Loretta Frances.
Skillet bread, sourdough, and vinegar pie : cooking in pioneer days /
by Loretta Frances Ichord.
p. cm.
Summary: Presents a look at what was eaten in the American West by pioneers on the trail, cowboys on cat-
tle drives, and gold miners in California camps, with available ingredients, cooking methods, and equipment.
Includes recipes and appendix of classroom cooking directions.
Includes bibliographical references and index.
ISBN 0-7613-1864-X (lib. bdg.)
1. Cookery, American—Juvenile literature. 2. Frontier and pioneer life—United States—Juvenile literature.
[1. Cookery, American—History. 2. United States—History—1849-1877. 3. Frontier and pioneer life.] I. Title.
TX715 .I22423 2003   641.5973—dc21   2002008157

Published by The Millbrook Press Inc.
2 Old New Milford Road, Brookfield, Connecticut 06804
www.millbrookpress.com

CONTENTS

Introduction 5

OREGON TRAIL PIONEERS
AND WHAT THEY ATE 7

Chapter 1
SLABS OF BACON AND
OTHER SUPPLIES 8
Bacon Cornbread 15

Chapter 2
GRIT AND BUGS IN THEIR FOOD 16
Skillet Bread 24 • Dried Apple Pie 26

FORTY-NINERS AND WHAT THEY ATE ❖ 29

Chapter 3
EATING ON THE RUN FOR THE GOLD 30
Sourdough Starter 36 • Sourdough Flapjacks 37

Chapter 4
FOREIGN FLAVORS, HOMEMADE PIES,
AND SOUTHERN COOKING COME TO THE MINES 38
Cornish Pasties 42

THE COWBOYS AND WHAT THEY ATE ❖ 45

Chapter 5
COOKIE RULES THE CHUCK WAGON 46
Vinegar Pie 50

Chapter 6:
JAVA, PRAIRIE STRAWBERRIES,
AND SKUNK EGGS 52
Chuck Wagon Beans 57

Appendix 58
Source Notes 59
Bibliography 61
Index 63

INTRODUCTION

When you hear the word "camping," you probably think of roasting marshmallows, cooking burgers and hot dogs over a fire, and sleeping in a cozy tent. But would camping be this much fun if you and your family had to do it every single day, for up to six straight months, in all kinds of weather, with limited food, water, and fuel? This is what the pioneers who traveled on the Oregon Trail in the mid-1800s faced.

Starting in 1843, large groups of pioneers left Independence, Missouri, in wagon trains and headed west to the Oregon Country (not officially a Territory until 1848). Each covered wagon, pulled by a team of oxen, moved at a rate of 2 miles (3.25 kilometers) per hour, so it took these emigrants six to seven months to cover just over 2,000 miles (3300 kilometers). Because it took so long, wagon trains had to leave in the early spring, no later than the beginning of May, to reach the mountain passes before snow blocked their way. Packing food, planning, and preparing six months of meals for their families was a major task for pioneer women. They knew there was no way to keep their food cool and there were few places on the trail to replenish their supplies. These pioneers were not the only ones who had trouble fixing meals in rugged circumstances. In 1849, when gold was discovered in California, it was mostly men who hurried across the Oregon Trail or sailed around South America and up the California coast to the goldfields. When these gold-seekers reached the rough mining camps, they had to fix their own meals out of a meager selection of food.

Then, after the American Civil War ended in 1865, another type of pioneer ventured out West. He was called a cowboy because he drove massive cattle herds from Texas to northern ranges. During these long, dusty trail rides, a male cook would follow in a chuck wagon full of food staples to use in preparing meals for the hungry cowboys.

Many pioneer men and women kept detailed journals of their day-to-day lives, and from these we have learned what was eaten and how these three groups of pioneers prepared meals in harsh environments.

The recipes included in this book use modern methods and equipment without losing any authentic taste. At the end of each recipe is a note describing how the meal was fixed in pioneer days. Since you'll be working with hot cooking appliances and sharp utensils, you will need an adult's assistance. To prepare the recipes for a class project, an appendix at the end of the book will tell you how to increase the ingredients.

So take a taste of what the pioneers ate when they opened up the West in America between 1843 and 1889.

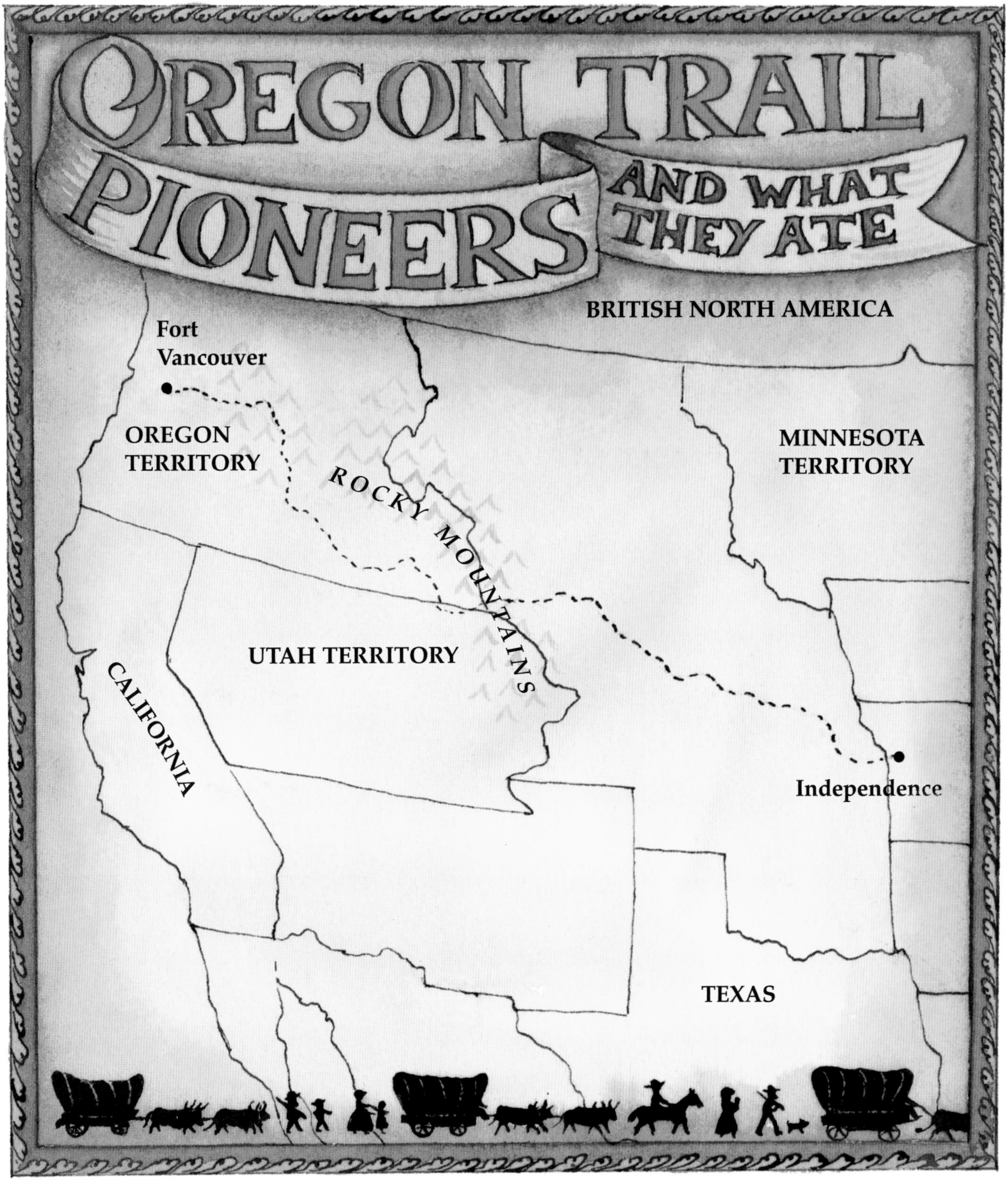

OREGON TRAIL PIONEERS

AND WHAT THEY ATE

BRITISH NORTH AMERICA

Fort
Vancouver

OREGON
TERRITORY

MINNESOTA
TERRITORY

ROCKY MOUNTAINS

UTAH TERRITORY

CALIFORNIA

Independence

TEXAS

1
SLABS of BACON AND OTHER SUPPLIES

Why would so many people in the mid-1800s decide to pack up, leave their homes in the eastern part of America, and, without a trustworthy map, make a long, hard journey west to the Oregon Country? There were many reasons, but the biggest one was the overcrowded conditions in the East, resulting in the shortage of good farming land.

Unhappy northeasterners had learned of the beautiful Oregon Country. An awesome wilderness, it stretched from the crest of the Rockies (a great chain of mountains in the West, extending from New Mexico all the way up to Canada) to the Pacific Coast and included the present states of Oregon, Washington, and Idaho. Tired of frigid winters, northeasterners were ready for a land with a mild climate and rich soil.

Their heads had been filled with tall tales of pigs waiting in Oregon Country, already cooked with forks and knives sticking in them, and pumpkins so big that a barn could be carved out of just one! Whole families loaded covered wagons with enough supplies to last them half a year and headed for this "promised land," where the lush ground was waiting for them.

Imagine trying to load a covered wagon with all your family's belongings and enough food for a six-month trip. The inside of a covered wagon was small, measuring 4 by 10 feet (1 by 3 meters). If you lay an average hall closet on its side, it would be about the same size as the bed of a covered wagon.

The pioneers had heard about the wildlife along the trail west, so they packed shotguns, muzzle-loading rifles, and fishing poles with folding rods into their wagons. But families didn't want to count on finding fresh meat every day, so they carried basic food staples as well. Some emigrants brought along their family cow for milk and butter. Others brought a "walking larder" of a few sheep, chickens, and a steer or two, using them in the first months of travel for meat and eggs. A few of the wealthier pioneers drove herds of cattle across the Oregon Trail, but often the animals were more trouble than they were worth. The cattle strayed, slowed down the wagon train, stampeded, and were sometimes stolen by Native American tribes.

FOOD SUPPLIES ⚙ The guidebooks recommended these amounts of food to take for each adult person: 200 pounds (91 kilograms) of flour, 75 pounds (34 kilograms) of bacon, 30 pounds (14 kilograms) of pilot bread (hardtack), 5 pounds (2 kilograms) of coffee, 2 pounds (1 kilogram) of tea, 25 pounds (11 kilograms) of sugar, half a bushel (18 liters) of dried beans, 10 pounds (4.5 kilograms) of rice, a bushel (35 liters) of dried fruit (mostly dried apples), 2 pounds (1 kilogram) of saleratus (baking soda), 10 pounds (4.5 kilograms) of salt, half a bushel (18 liters) of cornmeal, 15 pounds (7 kilograms) of parched or ground corn, one keg of vinegar, a few spices, and lemon extract.

Bacon: Besides bread, bacon was one of the most frequently eaten foods on the trail. The pioneers packed their bacon in strong 100-pound (45-kilogram) sacks or in boxes or barrels loaded with bran to keep it from spoiling. If the fat on the bacon was white, the bacon was good, but if the fat yellowed, then the meat had turned rancid and wormy. Piles of bacon, shaped like pyramids, were often seen lying along the Oregon Trail, dumped out because the fatty pork had gone bad or it had overloaded the wagon.

Coffee: Coffee was packed green. The coffee beans were roasted in a frying pan over the campfire and then ground in a coffee mill. The ground beans were put in a pot with water and set by the fire to brew. If the coffee beans ran out, the pioneers substituted parched corn, peas, barley, wheat, rye, or bran for their coffee.

10

Saleratus: This was an early baking soda. It was a chemical leavening, like baking soda today, that produced carbon dioxide gas to make breads rise without yeast and cakes without eggs. It had a stronger, more bitter taste than modern baking soda. Packaged in paper envelopes, it had to be mixed with an acidic (sour) food to activate the leavening process.

COOKING EQUIPMENT The overlanders chose their cooking utensils with care because the equipment had to withstand high temperatures over an open fire. Some pioneers packed sheet-iron cookstoves so they wouldn't have to cook over a fire, but the stoves were dead weight in the wagons and were often dumped on the trail.

A typical wagon heading west would have the following cooking equipment in its provision boxes (anything from a large basket to a trunk): spiders (cast-iron frying pans with legs), tin-plated cups, dinnerware, spoons, forks, a kettle, coffeepot, wooden rolling pin, wooden butter churn, coffee mill, tin and wooden pails, a keg for water, reflector oven, and a Dutch oven.

Reflector Oven: This medium-sized container was also called a tin-kitchen. It had a hooded dome on one side and was open on the other. The open side had shelves and could bake several pies and breads at the same time when placed by a campfire. It was lightweight and perfect for travel.

Dutch Oven: This round cast-iron pot with three legs and a lid was the most useful piece of cookware on the trail. It came in different sizes, and if a pioneer had more than one, the Dutch ovens could be stacked one on top of the other in the campfire. Inside was placed a stew, a roast, bread, or a pie. Anything that was normally baked in an oven at home could be baked in a Dutch oven on a campfire.

Water Keg: The most important container on the trip was the keg for carrying water. It was a daily chore on the trail to find fresh water to fill the sometimes 10-gallon (38-liter) kegs. No one wanted empty kegs of water at dinnertime because then only hardtack (a rock-hard, dry cracker) was served with nothing to wash it down. Many pioneers refer to these times in their journals as "drycamping."

The Oregon Trail followed along rivers like the Missouri, the Platte, the North Platte, the Sweetwater, and the Snake, so the emigrants could find running water. They called it "living water" because of the tapoles, worms, and moss found in it. But it was always a good sign if the "wigglers" were alive because it meant the water was safe to drink. Sometimes, along some stretches of the Oregon Trail, the only water around was under a sandy bed or in a muddy hole. The pioneers either drank the cloudy water as it was, used a cloth to strain the dirt out, or sprinkled cornmeal in the liquid to filter it. The worst bodies of water, found along some portions of the Platte River, were stagnant, covered with alkali (a substance that comes from certain soils. In water it is a basic [salty] solution that has a milky appearance, is slippery to touch, and has a bitter taste), and full of bacteria (from animal feces and latrines dug too close to the river). After getting sick from drinking this tainted water, the emigrants drank vinegar, considered an all-purpose drink, to cure the ills.

But vinegar didn't help those who became infected with cholera, a waterborne disease with high fever, vomiting, and diarrhea, contracted from drinking contaminated water. Nor did it help those suffering from dysentery (severe diarrhea) caused by eating rotting food, drinking dirty water, and not washing hands. No one knew at the time that boiling the water would have killed the bacteria. Those who drank only hot boiled coffee with their meals saved themselves, without knowing why, from cholera and dysentery, the two leading causes of death for thousands of the emigrants who came across the Oregon Trail during the 1800s.

Searching for water along the Oregon Trail did have its exciting moments. The natural springs that the overlanders came upon in Wyoming and Idaho delighted them. The Ice Springs Slough in Wyoming along the Sweetwater River was strange and fascinating. It was a marshy area where water collected, froze, and was kept insulated beneath a tundra-like soil. Despite its bad smell and alkaline (bitter) taste, the curious pioneers dug down one foot below the ground surface and gathered the ice to melt and use in cooking. Some of the men fixed themselves mint juleps by adding whiskey and wild mint that grew along the river to the ice. More unusual flows of water were found at Soda Springs, in what is now Idaho. The springs have naturally carbonated water. The emigrants fixed themselves lemonade with the bubbly water by mixing in lemon extract or vinegar with sugar. The fizzy drinks reminded them of the sodas back home. Another natural spring that drew a lot of attention was Beer Springs (now called Hooper Springs). The pioneers thought the gurgling water looked and tasted like small beer (watered-down beer).

BACON CORNBREAD

6–8 servings

You will need:

6 slices bacon
¾ cup white flour
1½ cups yellow cornmeal
4 teaspoons baking powder
½ teaspoon salt
2 eggs
1¼ cups milk
¼ cup bacon fat

Equipment:

frying pan
tongs and pot-holders
cutting board
measuring cups and spoons
8-inch by 12-inch baking pan
paper napkin
mixing bowl
wooden spoon
knife for chopping

What to do:

1. Preheat oven to 370°F.
2. Fry bacon slices until brown and crisp in frying pan. Take bacon out with tongs and set aside on cutting board.
3. Have adult tip frying pan and pour out ¼ cup bacon fat. Set aside. Grease baking pan with leftover bacon fat, using napkin.
4. Put all remaining ingredients, including ¼ cup bacon fat, into bowl and mix with wooden spoon until smooth.
5. With adult's help, chop bacon into small pieces and mix into batter.
6. Pour batter into baking pan and bake at 370°F for 30 minutes.
7. Take out of oven with pot-holders. Cut into squares and serve warm.

How Did the Pioneers Make Bacon Cornbread?

Ingredients: Instead of baking powder, saleratus was used. The milk came from the family cow. In the beginning of the journey, some pioneers packed eggs in the flour barrel or with a grain, like bran or oats. Others took live chickens with them or may have purchased eggs at the forts along the Oregon Trail. But eggs would have been a fragile cargo, so this recipe may have been made without them.

Equipment: The bacon was fried in a spider before it was added to the batter. The bread was then baked in a Dutch oven on a campfire. Hot coals were placed around the raised lip of the oven's cover. Careful attention had to be paid so the cornbread didn't scorch on the bottom.

GRIT AND BUGS 2 IN THEIR FOOD

Cooking a meal along the Oregon Trail was not like camping out beside a dust-free superhighway. The trail west was a group of wagon ruts in the ground that led the pioneers across the Great Plains (then called the Great American Desert), through rocky mountain passes, and over sandy western deserts. Prairie winds blew grit and bugs into everything. Between drinking mud in the water and eating sand in their food, the pioneers felt as if they had swallowed a "peck of dirt" (about 8 quarts or 9 liters) by the time they reached Oregon Country.

Fixing these gritty meals on the trail started at daybreak, around 4:00 A.M., when everyone rose and went about their tasks to break camp. The women squatted on the ground and busied themselves with making a fire and preparing breakfast, while the men did the heavier work of feeding the animals and hooking up the oxen to the wagons. If there were enough food supplies left or the hunting for wild game had been good, the overlanders ate well at the start of each day. They would sit on a box, the bare ground, or on top of an India rubber cloth (a waterproof material like our Gore-Tex™ water repellent fabric today) and eat johnnycakes, freshly baked bread, mush with milk, and fried meat. On other days breakfast was beans and bacon that had been slowly simmering overnight on the ashes of a campfire. Both adults and children drank hot coffee at every meal.

Around midday, the pioneers reined in their oxen, giving themselves and their livestock a rest for an hour. They referred to this stop as nooning. They didn't bother to start a campfire, so they ate what was left over from breakfast or munched on a sandwich made with bacon or beans.

In the evening when the wagon train halted for the night, the pioneer women prepared meals that took longer, like stews made with fresh game shot on the trail. After dinner was over, they often stayed up late at night to get breakfast preparations ready for the next morning.

MAKING A CAMPFIRE 🌐 How did the pioneer women make their campfires? First, they dug a shallow trench to shelter the flames from the wind. Fuel for the fires was usually collected at the nooning break by men, women, and children. Finding wood for fuel became more and more difficult once the pioneers had passed Fort Kearny, Nebraska. The forest started to disappear and a flat terrain with short-grass and very few trees took its place. Next to the common complaint in pioneer journals of "camped without water" or "drycamped" came another, "camped without wood." But with thousands of buffalo herds roaming the short-grass of the Great Plains west of Missouri and east of the Rockies, a new fuel

was discovered. Buffalo dung, shaped like flat saucers, could be found drying on the prairie. The dried dung, which became known as buffalo chips, ignited easily and burned with little smoke and no odor. Though children helped their parents gather the chips into sacks, some of the older kids had more fun throwing the chips at each other like Frisbee™ flying discs.

After the wagon train left the plains and went into the Rockies, where the buffalo didn't roam, mountain sagebrush was used for fuel instead of the trusty chips.

After gathering the fuel, digging a trench, and putting up poles to hang the cooking pots, the pioneers started the fire with friction matches, called lucifers. They were invented in 1827 and resembled the wooden matches we use today. Many of the emigrants didn't care for these early matches because, when jostled, the sticks would explode and give off a terrible sulfur-like odor, and if they got wet, they were useless. When the pioneers ran out of matches, another way of making a fire was to hold a small piece of thick glass on the ground and let the sun shine through until the heat generated a flame. If neither of these methods worked, a last desperate effort to get a fire going was to shoot a pistol at close range at a rag filled with gunpowder. Keeping a fire lit was even more difficult for the women whenever thunder and lightning struck the plains and hail rained down on their campfire and cooking preparations.

NATURE PROVIDED FOOD FOR THE CAMPFIRE ◙ Plant and animal life filled the Great Plains in the 1840s. Pioneers welcomed a change to their boring diet of bacon, bread, and dried apples. When they had time to stop and hunt, they shot fresh game like prairie chickens (grouse), prairie dogs, ducks, pronghorn antelope, jackrabbits, buffalo birds (they liked to perch on the backs of buffalo), and the mighty buffalo themselves. The pioneers fished for trout with their fishing poles, using grasshoppers or a piece of white cloth for bait.

Many journals recount the awesome sight of a rumbling brown mass of hairy, humpbacked animals racing across the plains. The North American buffalo (really a bison and part of the bovine breed) was immense! Some stood 6 feet (1.83 meters) high at the shoulders and weighed 1,800 to 2,000 pounds (810 to 900 kilograms).

After killing a buffalo, the pioneers ate the hump right away or cut it up and made it into jerky. Long strips were hung over poles or strung on ropes and laid over the wagon cover to dry. A buffalo tongue was considered a delicacy and was either pickled or smoked. Buffalo meat was darker and coarser than beef. The tough parts and the bones were made into soups, while the buffalo steaks were fried or broiled. Here are a few dishes created by the pioneers that are unlikely to be repeated today: Dried Buffalo Lung, Baked Buffalo Nose, Buffalo Intestines Filled with Grasses and Set in the Sun to Ferment, and Raw Buffalo Liver Sprinkled with Gall Bladder Juice.

When hunting for wild game on the trail, the pioneers would sometimes come across Native American tribes. In the flatlands, the tribes were buffalo hunters; west of the Rockies they were seed gatherers and small animal hunters; and in the Northwest they were salmon fishermen, hunters, and gatherers. These tribes, with different languages and ways of life, were generally helpful and not dangerous to the first groups of wagon trains coming through their lands. They often showed the emigrants the way to water, told them which wild plants were safe to eat, and traded needed foodstuffs, like fresh fish, for the pioneers' fishhooks, calico shirts, files, crackers, bread, beads, and buttons.

With this help from the tribes along the trail, the pioneers soon learned to spot delicious vegetation. Many times they simply leaned from their wagon seats and yanked up sprouting potherbs, wild onions, garlic, and dandelions for salads and tea. Wild grapes, strawberries, gooseberries, cranberries, and salal berries were eaten right on the spot or saved to bake in pies.

BAKING BREAD AND PIES OVER A CAMPFIRE 🌀 Though the wind on the trail often blew mosquitoes and sand into the bread dough, baking was done every day over an open fire, no matter what the weather. Bread was the number one food eaten on the Oregon Trail and sometimes the only thing, when supplies ran low during the last leg of the journey or when travel was so hurried there wasn't time to fix a meal. Quick breads (made without yeast), like skillet bread and bread-on-a-stick, were baked often because they didn't take long. Bread-on-a-stick was made by mixing water and flour right in the flour sack. A stick was then placed into the bag and twisted in the wet dough until some stuck to the end. Then it was placed in the ground by the fire and turned a few times to keep it from burning.

Yeast breads took longer to make because packaged active dry yeast was not available until after 1870. Before that time, pioneers had to make a starter of wild yeast (a microscopic plant that travels in the air) by putting equal amounts of flour and water or flour and milk into a container. The mixture was set out to ferment (when yeast plant cells begin to grow and the batter gets puffy and bubbly) in the warmest part of a covered wagon. This mixture, called a starter, was used to make salt-rising bread, a fine-grained loaf with a cheesy flavor, and other types of yeast breads. Saleratus (a chemical leavening) was added to these breads because the unstable wild yeast (a biological leavening) couldn't be depended on to make the bread rise.

In addition to bread, lots of fruit pies, either baked or fried, were cooked on the way to Oregon Country. Wild berries were used when available, but most of the pie fillings were made with the dried apples, pumpkin, peaches, and currants brought along on the trip. Fresh fruit was too heavy and perishable to be carried in the wagons. Dried apple pies were made so often that the pioneers grew tired of them and made up this ditty:

> *Spit in my ear, tell me lies,*
> *But give me no dried apple pies!*

COOKING ON INDEPENDENCE DAY! ❦ By the time the overlanders had reached Independence Rock (a giant granite boulder on the plains of the Sweetwater Valley in Wyoming), they had replenished their food supplies at Fort Laramie at great expense. Forty pounds (18 kilograms) of rice, costing $3.00 in Missouri, sold for $90 to $190 at the fort. But if they had arrived at the Rock on or around the Fourth of July, they were ready to celebrate. It meant they were on schedule and would reach Oregon Country before the snows hit. As deer and other game meat roasted and as cakes, pies, and yeast breads baked, the pioneers entertained themselves by climbing up on Independence Rock to carve their names on its

surface. Many of these names can still be seen on the rock, called the Giant Register of the Desert.

Some emigrants decided to go farther, passing Independence Rock to camp closer to South Pass, where the Oregon Trail crossed the Rockies. They celebrated on the Fourth by gathering early snow off the ground and mixing it with milk, calling this delicious dessert Sweetwater Mountain Ice Cream.

These stopovers refreshed the emigrants before they started the hardest part of their journey, the last leg. After leaving the Rockies, they chose either to cross the Blue Mountains in eastern Oregon or the Cascade Mountains to the west. Many of the pioneers who had made it over the eastern mountains constructed rafts by taking the wheels off their wagons and putting them on top of logs tied together. They then traveled down the mighty Columbia River, to the rich farmland of the Willamette Valley to pursue their dreams of settling in the West.

SKILLET BREAD

8 servings

You will need:
3½ cups unbleached all-purpose flour
1 teaspoon salt
1 teaspoon baking powder
1 teaspoon baking soda
3 tablespoons butter
1½ cups buttermilk
Flour for kneading
Butter for greasing skillet

Equipment:
measuring cups and spoons
mixing bowl
wooden spoon
table fork
wooden or plastic board
9-inch cast-iron skillet
2 pot-holders

What to do:
1. Preheat oven to 400°F.
2. Mix all the dry ingredients together in bowl.
3. Add butter and cut into flour mixture with fork until it looks grainy, like cornmeal.
4. Stir in buttermilk.
5. Sprinkle flour on board and knead dough a few times with your hands, folding, pulling, and shaping.
6. Rub butter along sides and bottom of skillet.
7. Place dough in skillet and push it to fill the pan.
8. Place skillet in oven and bake for 30 minutes or until the surface of the bread has risen and is light brown in color. Have an adult lift the very hot skillet from oven with pot-holders and turn bread out of pan onto board. It will look like a giant biscuit.
9. Slice in wedge-shapes and serve with butter.

How Did the Pioneers Make Skillet Bread?

Ingredients: Flour in pioneer days was not bleached white like the all-purpose flour we have today. The chemical bleaching technique was not invented until the early 1900s. The overlanders used one of three types of flour: shorts, middlings, or superfine. The first two were not favorites because they contained the roughest part of the bran and wheat germ. Superfine flour was ground between two stones and then sifted to get out the coarse parts of the grain. It was closest to what we have today.

Saleratus was used instead of baking soda and baking powder. When the overlanders ran out of the commercial saleratus (sodium bicarbonate), they gathered it at the banks of natural soda springs found by the Sweetwater River in Wyoming and Idaho. Pieces were broken off the dried, white, crusty beds and mixed into the batter to make the bread rise.

These pioneers discovered a shortcut to making butter without using their butter churns. A can filled with cream was hung from the back of the wagon. The bumpy ride shook the can so hard that large balls of butter formed. The buttermilk (milk that is left after butter is churned) was separated from the butter balls and put in this recipe.

Equipment: A spider or Dutch oven was used to cook this bread. The dough was often kneaded right inside the cooking pan. The skillet or Dutch oven was then placed on the fire and hot coals were placed on its lid. The cook had to be careful not to get the fire too hot or the bread would burn on the outside and be raw in the middle.

DRIED APPLE PIE

6–8 Servings

You will need:

For the filling:
4 cups dried apples
2 cups granulated sugar
1 teaspoon ground cinnamon
1 tablespoon unbleached all-purpose
 flour

For the crust:
3 cups unbleached all-purpose flour
1 teaspoon salt
1 cup (2 sticks) butter
$\frac{1}{3}$ cup cold water
Butter for greasing

Equipment:

4-quart cooking pot
measuring cups and spoons
slotted spoon
2 mixing bowls
wooden spoon
small knife and one table fork
rolling pin
wooden board dusted with flour
9-inch pie plate
2 pot-holders

What to do:

Filling:
1. Fill cooking pot halfway up with water and boil.
2. Shut off heat and drop dried apple slices into freshly boiled water; soak them for 30 minutes.
3. When apple slices are soft, use slotted spoon to remove from water and place in mixing bowl.
4. Use the wooden spoon to mix apples with sugar, cinnamon, and 1 tablespoon of flour. Set aside.
5. Preheat oven to 425°F.

Crust:
6. Mix 3 cups flour and one teaspoon of salt in other mixing bowl with fork.
7. Add butter and cut into flour with fork until it looks coarse, like cornmeal.
8. Add $\frac{1}{3}$ cup cold water and mix with fork; shape dough with hands into a ball. Divide dough in half.
9. Use rolling pin on floured board to roll out half of dough to 2 inches wider than pie pan and $\frac{1}{8}$ inch thick.
10. Grease pie plate with butter.

11. Fold dough over and place in pan, unfolding it to line pie pan. Trim off any dough hanging over edge of pan with knife.
12. Spoon apple slices into pie pan. Set aside.
13. Dust board with more flour. Roll out second half of dough 2 inches bigger than pie pan and $\frac{1}{8}$ inch thick. Place on top of pie filling. Crimp (pinch) crust all around with fingers and make a vent by carving the letter A (for apple) in top of crust with knife.
14. Bake at 425°F for 15 minutes; then lower heat to 350°F and continue baking for another 25 minutes until pie is nicely browned. Have adult remove pie from oven with pot-holders. Let cool before cutting into wedges for serving.

How Did the Pioneers Make Dried Apple Pie?

Ingredients: The above ingredients would have been carried in the wagon. Cinnamon sticks (ground into a powder for this recipe) were packed in the provision box. Sugar in the nineteenth century came in the form of loaves or cones. The emigrants had to purchase crushed sugar from these heavy loaves so as not to overload their wagons.

Equipment: Rolling out the pie crust was done on a wagon seat or on top of a provision box. If a rolling pin wasn't available, then the cook used her hands to shape the dough. Pies were baked in a Dutch oven placed on top of hot coals with more coals put on its lid to brown the crust. A reflector oven or simply a sheet of tin arranged around the fire to reflect heat onto the pie could also have been used.

FORTY-NINERS
AND WHAT THEY ATE

NORTH
AMERICA

California

SOUTH
AMERICA

3 EATING ON THE RUN FOR THE $ GOLD

An amazing thing happened at a sawmill in California on January 24, 1848. Gold was discovered! A carpenter named James Marshall found a piece of gold about half the size of a pea in the water at Sutter's Mill. Word spread fast. Thousands of men left their families behind in the East to hurry across the Oregon Trail. But instead of heading for the Oregon Territory, they took the California cutoff and rushed through a dry, thirsty desert and over an awesome range of mountains, called the Sierras, to reach the goldfields. They had hopes of striking it rich and sending for their wives and children or going back home with sacks of gold dust. Many of these men were city-bred and had no knowledge of how to drive a team of oxen pulling a wagon. Many had never hunted for food, cooked outdoors, or done any kind of hard physical labor. In their haste to get going, some men bumped into trees and turned over their rigs. These gold-seekers became known as forty-niners because this stampede of pioneers started westward in 1849.

Those who took the overland route to reach California had the same problem as earlier pioneers—overloaded wagons. The miners began to call Fort Laramie "Camp Sacrifice" because of the tons of supplies that were dumped off the wagons at the fort. Barrels of bread, stacks of bacon, shovels, and stoves were taken off to lighten the wagons before crossing over the Rockies. However, in 1850, some men were in such a hurry to reach the goldfields that they ended up packing too little, depending on other overlanders to give them food. This behavior set off a tide of starvation that killed many people on the trail in 1850.

In 1849 and the following ten years, so many travelers went on the Oregon Trail that the plains suffered from a traffic jam of people who hunted and killed many of the area's creatures. Also, the livestock that the emigrants brought with them stripped the Great Plains of vegetation. Thousands of buffalo were shot for sport and left to rot, taking away the Plains Indians' way of life and food supply. By the late 1800s, fewer than 500 buffalo were left in existence. Some pioneers even shot Native Americans, causing bad feelings to develop among the tribes toward the white man.

Not all gold-seekers traveled by land; thousands came by way of ship, making a 15,000-mile (24,000-kilometer) journey around the tip of South America that took five months. There was no refrigeration on board, so the sea biscuits (hardtack) became wormy and the other foods, like salted meat, rice, beans, potatoes, salted pork, and turnips, became foul. Vinegar and molasses were used to kill the taste of rotting food and bad water on board.

Those who wanted to shorten their journey by sea chose to stop at the Isthmus of Panama (there was no Panama Canal at the time). There they crossed a tropical, 70-mile (113-kilometer) land bridge between the Atlantic and Pacific Oceans to catch another ship heading up to California.

While traveling through this jungle on mules and in canoes, the pioneers ate foods like baked monkey and grilled iguana, cooked by the natives living in the area. These prospectors faced the same risks of contracting cholera and dysentery from eating and drinking contaminated food and water that the overlanders faced. Also, they had the added danger of becoming infected with malaria (a sometimes fatal disease causing chills, fever, and sweating) from the mosquitoes living in the jungle.

When these forty-niners finally arrived in California and made their way to the Mother Lode (a large area in the hills between the Sierra Mountains and the valleys of California where great deposits of gold were found), they were both tired and happy. But they soon discovered that holding a pan (an iron container about 18 inches [46 centimeters] across and 4 inches [10 centimeters] deep) and moving it around and around in a cold mountain stream to separate a small amount of gold from sand, gravel, and water was backbreaking work.

Early mining camps, called tent cities, were located along the rivers. They had limited food supplies. Since the prospectors didn't have easy access to fresh fruits and vegetables, many suffered from malnutrition and scurvy (a serious disease caused by a lack of vitamin C that can be fatal if left untreated). A miner's diet was especially poor when he was down on his luck and had nothing to eat but hardtack and jerky. One miner, E. G. Buffram, wrote about suffering from bleeding gums, swollen limbs, and broken blood vessels, which are symptoms of scurvy. He saved his own life by eating wild bean sprouts he discovered growing by his camp. Another miner, John Doble, wrote in his 1851 journal about picking a panful of succulent California lettuce, growing along gulches and on the flats in the springtime. He was referring to miner's lettuce (*Montia perfoliata*), a wild, sweet-tasting lettuce, full of vitamin C. It can be found today, as it was growing then, in cool mountain areas and foothills in California during the spring.

The Native Americans living around the mining camps helped many hungry miners find wild herbs and berries that were safe to eat and told them where to fish for the best trout and hunt for raccoon.

A miner had to wash 160 pans in the streams to come up with enough gold flakes, nuggets, or gold dust to be worth $16.00, the average price of an ounce of gold. If he had a sack of gold (gold dust was used for money), then he could go to a store, often a tent, in one of the mining towns that had cropped up around the camps and purchase a supply of preserved foods like pickles, dried fruits, split peas, dried beans, raisins, bacon, flour, sugar, cheese, cornmeal, lard, and canned meats. Everything was expensive. Wheat flour sold for as high as $1.50 a pound. A loaf of bread that sold for four cents in New York sold for seventy-five cents at the mines. Eggs cost as much as $1.00 to $3.00 apiece; apples, $1.00 to $5.00 each; coffee, $5.00 a pound. If a miner really struck it rich, he might travel to one of the eateries in Hangtown (first known as Dry Diggins, then

Hangtown, and now Placerville) and order a greasy dish called Hangtown Fry. This "status symbol" meal consisted of fried eggs, fried oysters, and bacon, costing around $7, a fortune for the times.

Besides eateries, saloons and gambling houses shot up in many towns to help the miners lose their hard-earned gold. Alcoholic drinks served at these establishments were given creative names like firewater, bug juice, cactus juice, gut warmer, Kansas sheep-dip, tarantula juice, and tonsil varnish.

Back in camp, away from restaurants and stores, miners had to learn to cook and season their own foods from sparse supplies. When they wanted to spice up their meals and had run out of salt, they sprinkled gunpowder on their food (*not* a tasty substitute). They also made a lot of flapjacks (pancakes, also called slapjacks and flippers), because they were easy and needed only a few ingredients.

When miners had more time on Sundays (their usual day off from mining), they brought out their sourdough starter (a bubbly mixture of fermented wild yeast, flour, and water or milk) to give extra punch to their flapjacks and to bake sourdough bread in Dutch ovens.

If a prospector didn't have a skillet to cook with, he used his gold pan. Besides sifting for gold in the pans, miners used them to wash their clothes, feed their mules, and cook their meals.

SOURDOUGH STARTER

You will need:
1 cup warm water
1 tablespoon sugar
1 cup unbleached all-purpose flour
4 tablespoons buttermilk

Equipment:
measuring cup and spoons
clean glass quart jar with lid
wooden spoon
dish towel

What to do:
1. Pour warm water (85°F) into glass jar. (Never use plastic, metal, or aluminum containers. The dough will react with them and the taste will be ruined.)
2. Add sugar, flour, and buttermilk. Stir with wooden spoon.
3. Cover top of jar with towel.
4. Set jar on top of a water heater or other warm place for 2 to 3 days or until it smells sour and looks like bubbly pancake batter.
5. If a clear liquid rises to the top of the starter, stir it back in.
6. Put lid on and close tightly. Place jar in refrigerator until ready to use in biscuit, bread, or pancake recipes.
7. Before using in a recipe, take starter out of refrigerator and let stand at room temperature for several hours.
8. After taking out a portion of starter for a recipe, replace it by putting the same amount of water and flour back in jar (this is called feeding the starter). For example: If 1½ cups of starter was used in a recipe, put 1½ cups of flour and 1½ cups of warm water in leftover starter. Mix, let sit for 2 to 3 hours, and return to refrigerator.

If starter is not used very often, it can stay in the refrigerator indefinitely as long as it is fed and kept alive by taking a cup of the starter out and replacing it with more flour and liquid every week or so.

How Did the Forty-Niners Make Sourdough Starter?

Ingredients: Miners often just mixed flour, water, and sugar together and let the mixture sit in a warm place to make their sourdough starter. Milk and butter were rarely available in the mining camps. The miners' starters differed from the wild yeast mixtures made by the overlanders because the prospectors used their starters over and over again by feeding them. A sourdough starter could be kept alive for years, and some miners believed it got better with age.

Equipment: A small wooden cask with a lid or a jug or crock made out of pottery was the type of container the miners would have used to store their sourdough starter.

SOURDOUGH FLAPJACKS

4–6 servings

You will need:
1½ cups sourdough starter
3 cups unbleached all-purpose flour
1 cup warm (85°F) water
1 tablespoon sugar
¼ teaspoon salt
½ teaspoon baking soda
1 tablespoon baking powder
1 cup milk
2 eggs
¼ cup vegetable oil

vegetable oil spray
brown sugar

Equipment:
measuring cups and spoons
2-quart glass mixing bowl
wooden spoon
dish towel
10-inch skillet or griddle
metal spatula

What to do:
1. Sourdough Sponge: The night before making flapjacks, take the sourdough starter from refrigerator and allow it to come to room temperature.
2. Then measure out 1½ cups of sourdough starter and put in glass mixing bowl. Put the rest of the starter back in the refrigerator. Add 1½ cups of the unbleached, all-purpose flour and 1 cup warm water to the bowl. Mix well, cover bowl with towel, and let sit overnight unrefrigerated. This is called proofing—making a very sour sponge by spreading the wild yeast throughout the dough.
3. The next day measure out 2 cups of proofed sourdough sponge. Pour the leftover sponge into refrigerated starter jar. Then return the 2 cups of sponge to glass bowl and add the remaining flour, other dry ingredients, milk, eggs, and vegetable oil. Let rest for 15 minutes.
4. Spray vegetable oil on griddle or skillet and heat on medium high until drops of water sprinkled on griddle jump around. Have adult help to pour batter onto skillet in 4-inch-wide cakes and cook on medium heat until bubbles form. Turn each flapjack over with spatula and cook on the other side.
5. Serve with brown sugar.

How Did the Forty-Niners Make Sourdough Flapjacks?

Ingredients: For everyday flapjacks, miners just mixed flour and water together and fried them in pork fat. But if they wanted their cakes light and airy and if they had found some eggs at a store or farm, they made sourdough flapjacks. Saleratus would have been used in the place of modern-day baking powder and soda. Milk in the early 1850s was becoming more available because hotels and restaurants close to the camps were buying more cows. Brown sugar, a common sweetener of the time, was eaten on flapjacks and poured in the miners' coffee.

Equipment: The batter was mixed in a clay pitcher. A black iron skillet or a gold pan would have been used to cook the flapjacks. A miner turned the flapjacks over by lifting and tilting the skillet or pan until the pancakes flipped over.

FOREIGN FLAVORS, HOMEMADE PIES
AND SOUTHERN COOKING
COME TO THE MINES

Gold-seekers from Chile, Peru, and the scrublands of northern Mexico were the first of the foreign miners to arrive in California to pan for gold in 1848 and 1849. Many of them were experienced placer (gold deposits near the surface) miners. The Chinese, Hawaiians, Australians, and Europeans had longer journeys by sea to reach the goldfields. These people of different cultures brought foreign flavors to the cooking in the mining camps.

The Chinese stood out more than the other foreigners because of their facial features, long braids (called queues), and baggy clothing. They suffered severely from prejudice and were forced off claims and turned away from jobs. But they survived these hardships and managed to find abandoned gold diggings where they searched for nuggets that others had missed. Some Chinese did find work as cooks in the mining towns.

Others started truck gardens on small pieces of land to grow the crisp, succulent vegetables important to their cooking, like bean sprouts, bamboo shoots, snow peas, and water chestnuts. They cooked nightly meals for themselves in clay pots full of vegetables, noodles, and slivers of sausage or pork, seasoned with herbs, or made simpler dishes of dried fish and shrimp served with herbal tea. The smells and sounds coming from the Chinese camps aroused a great curiosity in the other miners. But it wasn't until long after the Gold Rush ended that this delicious Chinese cuisine was finally accepted and enjoyed by all Americans.

After 1849, the gold deposits in the streams and surface rocks ran out, and miners had to start digging into the mountains. More men were needed, so mining for gold became a group activity instead of one for individuals. Hundreds of men from Cornwall, England, famous for their experience in hard-rock and deep-shaft mining, began sailing to California in the early 1850s. They became known as Cousin Jacks, because whenever a Cornishman learned of a job opening in the California mines, he would say, "I've got this cousin, Jack, who's looking for work!" The Cousin Jacks brought with them a taste for a baked meat-and-potato pie called a pasty. When they took their pasties down into the

mines, they were always careful to leave the last bite for the Tommyknockers, leprechaun-like creatures that no one ever saw. Though Tommyknockers might be either friend or foe to a hard-rock miner, the hope was that if a bite of pasty was left for them, they would warn the miner about any impending disaster in the shaft.

Besides the foreign and American men who arrived in California during the gold rush, a small number of women came to the mines, some with their husbands and others alone. A census taken in 1850 found that 73 percent of California's population was between the ages of twenty and forty, and 92 percent were males. The women who formed the remaining 8 percent found new freedoms and opportunities in the West, especially if they could cook. Miners missed home-cooked meals, and they would pay anything for a tender pie made by a woman's hand. One good cook by the name of Lucy Stoddard Wakefield arrived in California, divorced her husband, moved to Placerville, and started making pies. She made 240 pies a week and sold each pie for one dollar. Another woman, Mrs. Phelps, brought a cooking stove and two cows. She sold pies and also charged a dollar for a pint of milk, a rare treat.

Thousands of African-American men came to California in 1849 to try their luck as well. Some of the most educated, daring, and successful of the pioneers to come out of California's gold rush were African-

American. Many came as slaves with their masters, though quite a few ended up buying their freedom with gold dust ($1,000 was the amount necessary). Others came as freedmen who used gold to free their families. One black man, George Washington Dennis, came from Alabama in 1849 and after much hard work was able to buy his own and his mother's freedom. She started a business cooking southern foods for the miners and made $200 a day. Her son used the money to amass a fortune buying real estate in San Francisco.

The California gold rush lasted ten years. Dreams of riches came true only for a few. Some miners went back home empty-handed, but a larger number stayed in California to go into other types of work, such as logging, farming, ranching, and retailing. They created a state (California became the thirty-first state in the Union on September 9, 1850) with an exciting blend of cultures and foods from all over the world.

CORNISH PASTIES
4 Servings

You will need:

For the crust:
2 cups unbleached all-purpose
    flour
$1/2$ teaspoon salt
$2/3$ cup solid vegetable shortening
$1/2$ cup cold water
flour to dust work surface

For the filling:
$3/4$ pound ground chuck
$1/2$ cup chopped onion
$1/2$ cup grated rutabaga
2 cups diced potatoes
$1\frac{1}{2}$ teaspoons salt
$1/2$ teaspoon pepper

$1/3$ cup chopped fresh parsley or 2 tablespoons
    dried parsley
milk to brush pasties
cooking oil spray

Equipment:
measuring cups and spoons
large mixing bowl and wooden spoon
table fork
cutting board
plastic wrap
rolling pin
pastry brush
two cookie sheets and metal spatula
small knife
two pot-holders

What to do:
Crust:
1. Put flour into mixing bowl with salt. Add shortening and cut in with fork until texture of flour is like cornmeal.
2. Add water and mix with fork.
3. Turn out onto floured board. Knead dough with hands for a few seconds until well blended. Form into 4 balls, cover each one with plastic wrap, and chill in refrigerator for at least 2 hours.
4. Preheat oven to 375°F.

Filling:

5. Wash out bowl. Mix ground chuck, onions, rutabaga, potatoes, salt, pepper, and parsley together in bowl with wooden spoon.
6. Take dough out of refrigerator and roll out each ball into an 8-inch (20-centimeter) circle with rolling pin on floured cutting board.
7. Brush the edges of each circle of dough with milk using the pastry brush.
8. Place one cup of filling on one half of each circle and fold the other half over it. Seal the edges by pressing with a fork.
9. After assembling, lift each pasty with spatula off board and transfer to cookie sheet that is lightly sprayed with cooking oil. Place two on each cookie sheet.
10. With small knife cut ½-inch slits on top of each pasty to let out steam. Brush each pasty with milk.
11. Bake in 375°F oven for 45 minutes or until pasties are golden brown. Have adult remove cookie sheets from oven with pot-holders. Cut pasty in half to eat.

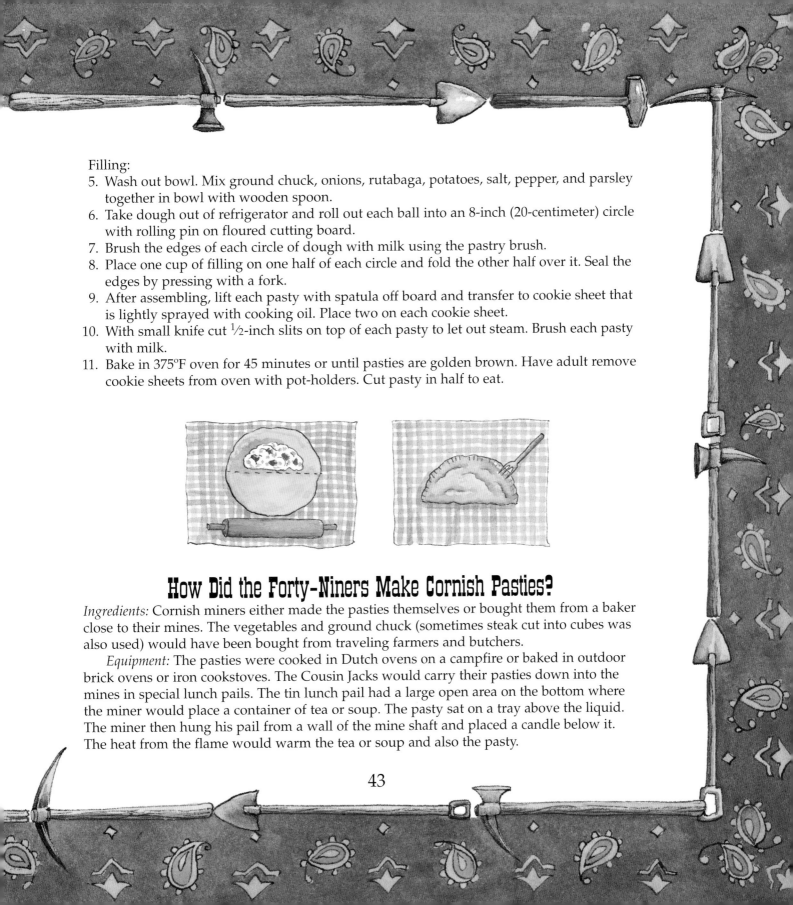

How Did the Forty-Niners Make Cornish Pasties?

Ingredients: Cornish miners either made the pasties themselves or bought them from a baker close to their mines. The vegetables and ground chuck (sometimes steak cut into cubes was also used) would have been bought from traveling farmers and butchers.

Equipment: The pasties were cooked in Dutch ovens on a campfire or baked in outdoor brick ovens or iron cookstoves. The Cousin Jacks would carry their pasties down into the mines in special lunch pails. The tin lunch pail had a large open area on the bottom where the miner would place a container of tea or soup. The pasty sat on a tray above the liquid. The miner then hung his pail from a wall of the mine shaft and placed a candle below it. The heat from the flame would warm the tea or soup and also the pasty.

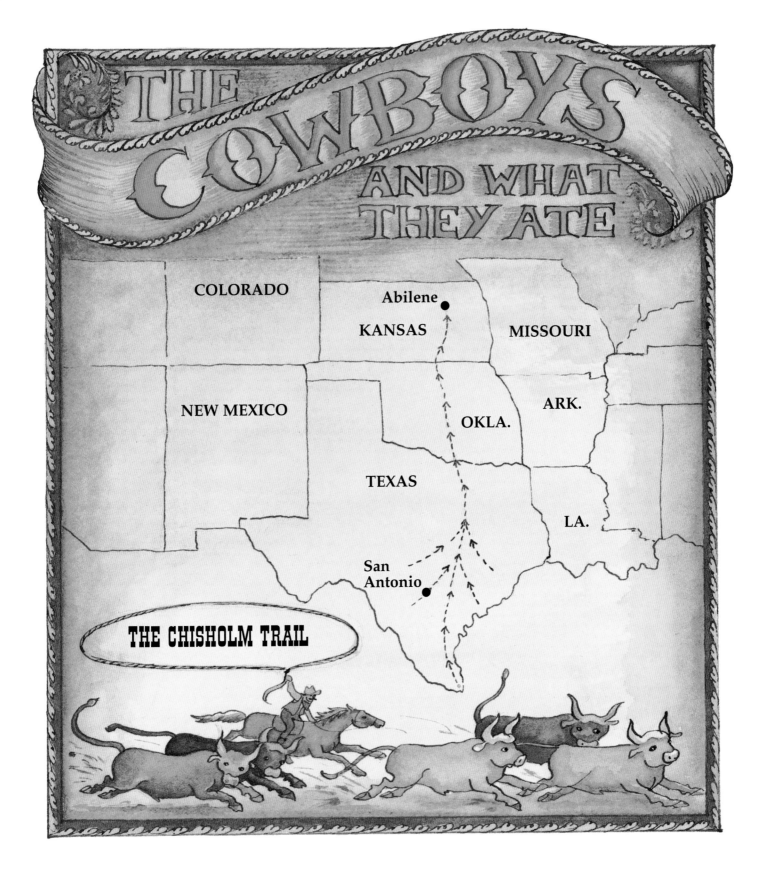

After the American Civil War ended in 1865, a new kind of pioneer went out West. He became known as a cowboy. His job was to drive large herds of longhorn cattle from Texas north to the newly built railroad in Abilene, Kansas. From there the cattle were sent on trains back East, where the demand for beef was great and very profitable. Several trails were used to drive cattle out of Texas, but one of the most famous was the Chisholm Trail. To herd over a thousand head of cattle on the Chisholm Trail was every pioneer boy's dream. The ones that did go were mostly teenagers or young men. These cowboys were of many nationalities and races, including Mexican, Spanish, Native American, and African-American.

When these herdsmen were on lonely trail drives full of dust and hard work, their appetites grew as big as the distances they traveled. So a cook was hired by the owner of a cattle company to feed his trail hands three square meals a day. This meal-handler drove a special outfit called a chuck (cowboy word for food) wagon and was called "Cookie" or "Miss Sally" by the cowboys he fed. He was usually an older man whose days of riding a mustang and herding cattle were over. Many of these cooks were known for their cranky dispositions, due to working long hours, from before daybreak to sundown, on meals for fifteen to twenty hungry cowboys in harsh weather conditions with limited supplies and equipment. The cook also served as camp dentist, doctor, referee for a foot race or a fight, mender of ripped clothes or saddles, banker, gravedigger, and repairman of anything that needed fixing.

Cookie's word was law when it came to his chuck wagon and the area 60 feet (18 meters) around it. Here are several of his rules of cowboy etiquette expected on the trail: No cowboy was allowed to ride into camp on his horse or tie the animal to the wheel of the chuck wagon or anywhere close to it. The cook didn't want dust blown in the food he was preparing, nor did he want horse hair in his beans. No one headed for the chuck wagon until Cookie shouted "Come an' get it!" No man was to leave food on his plate. If he couldn't finish his food, which was rare, then it was his responsibility to feed the scraps to the wildlife or put them in the squirrel can (a garbage can kept by the cook). Dirty plates were always dumped in the chuck pan (dishpan) under the mess-box lid and not left for the cook to pick up. If a visitor, not working with the outfit, stopped by to eat and talk, he was welcomed. But when the eating was done and the others had gone back to work, the stranger was expected to pick up the flour-sack towel and help Cookie with the dishes. And, finally, no cowboy was allowed to look through Cookie's wagon, messing up his organized supplies. However, the cook did allow a cowboy to help himself to a can of tomatoes to quench his thirst (canned foods were developed in 1810, but did not come into widespread use until after the Civil War).

The cook's chuck wagon was similar to other covered wagons, but it had a large water barrel, toolbox, coffee grinder, and a chuck box attached to it. The chuck box sat in the back of the wagon and was stationary. It had a back panel with a swinging leg that let down and formed a table where Cookie prepared the meals, but no one was allowed to use it for a dining table. The chuck box had lots of drawers and cubby holes where pots, pans, utensils, tin plates, cups, and smaller food items were kept. Larger spaces were left for the sourdough keg (the most precious of all the chuck wagon's cargo), flour, coffee, sugar, beans, rice, dried fruit, and lard. One special drawer was called the "possibles drawer" because it contained everything from sewing needles, buttons, razors, and castor oil to a bottle of whiskey for medicinal purposes. Underneath the chuck box was a hinged smaller box, called the boot, that contained heavier cooking pots like Dutch ovens and skillets. Directly below the wagon bed was the "possum belly," a stretched piece of cowhide that was filled with cow chips (dried cow dung) or wood in case the next camp didn't have any handy fuel available (finding fuel was always a problem). In addition to food-related supplies and grain for its team of horses or mules, the wagon also carried all the cowboys' gear like bedrolls, lanterns, slickers, ropes, and guns.

When good fuel was found for the campfire and all the cook's rules were being strictly followed, then he could concentrate on his baking. Sourdough biscuits cooked in a Dutch oven were his specialty and a number one necessity as far as the cowboys were concerned. They didn't care for any other kind of bread with their meals. In order to keep those biscuits coming, Cookie guarded his sourdough keg with his life and took it to bed with him every night wrapped in a blanket to keep it warm and alive. No sourdough made for a bad-tempered cook and an unhappy crew!

If all was going well on the trail ride and the meal-handler was in a good mood, he sometimes fixed a simple dessert called Spotted Pup for the men in the evening. It was made of cooked rice, raisins, and brown sugar. Rarely did he make pies, but if he had the right supplies on hand and was happy with the cowboys, then he might bake a few, making the tired cowboys want to kick up their heels in glee!

49

VINEGAR PIE

6–8 servings

You will need:

For the crust:
1½ cups unbleached all-purpose flour
½ teaspoon salt
½ cup butter (1 stick)
3 tablespoons cold water

For the filling:
2 eggs
½ cup white sugar
½ cup brown sugar
¼ cup unbleached all-purpose flour
⅛ teaspoon nutmeg

3 tablespoons cider vinegar
1 cup water
¼ cup melted butter

Equipment:

measuring cups and spoons
2-quart mixing bowl
wooden spoon
table fork
wooden board
rolling pin
9-inch pie pan
1-quart mixing bowl
2 pot-holders

What to do:

Crust: 1. Mix 1½ cups flour and ½ teaspoon salt in 2-quart mixing bowl. Cut butter into flour with fork until mixture looks like cornmeal. Pour in water and mix with hands, forming dough into a ball. Using rolling pin, roll out dough on floured board to 2 inches (5 centimeters) wider than pie pan and ⅛ inch (⅓ centimeter) thick. Fold dough in half and place in middle of pie pan and unfold it to line pan and spread along its sides. Set aside.
2. Preheat oven to 400°F.

Filling: 3. In 1-quart mixing bowl, beat two eggs with fork. Set aside.
4. Wash the 2-quart mixing bowl, then reuse to blend both sugars, ¼ cup flour, and nutmeg with fingers until there are no lumps.
5. Add vinegar, melted butter, beaten eggs, and 1 cup of water and stir with wooden spoon until well mixed.
6. Pour into pie shell and bake in oven at 400°F for 30 minutes.
7. Have adult remove from oven with pot-holders and let cool until firm enough to slice.

How Did the Cowboy Cook Make Vinegar Pie?

Ingredients: A cook on the trail was often an expert at baking vinegar pies. The pastry was called a "poor man's pie" because it was a substitute for lemon pie when none of the yellow fruit was at hand. If Cookie didn't have eggs or butter, which was often the case, he prepared this pie in the following way: To make the filling, he mixed a quarter-pint of vinegar (usually cider) with a half-pint of water and added sugar to taste. He then put a large lump of lard in his iron skillet and a little flour. The vinegar mixture was added to the skillet and boiled until thick, like gravy. He poured this mixture into a dough-lined pie pan and placed a crust on top. Most pioneers made vinegar pie with no top crust, as in the above recipe, but cowboys didn't care for topless pies, calling them "calf-slobber" or "boggy top" pies. So Cookie rolled out a top crust made of lots of lard and flour to cover the pie or he criss-crossed strips of dough over the filling. If a full top crust was used, the cook cut the cattle company's brand in it to let the steam out.

    Equipment: Cookie rolled out his pie dough with a beer bottle, since he didn't carry a rolling pin in his chuck wagon. After assembling the pie in a tin pie pan, he placed it inside a warming Dutch oven on the fire, covering it with a lid. Coals were put on the lid to brown the top.

6 JAVA, PRAIRIE STRAWBERRIES, AND SKUNK EGGS

Besides tender sourdough biscuits and the occasional dessert, the staple foods served from the chuck wagon were beans, canned peaches and tomatoes, beef jerky, and any wild game shot by the cowboys. All this grub was washed down with plenty of coffee (Java).

A typical routine of meals on the trail began with Cookie rolling out of his bedroll at three o'clock in the morning to fix the fire and start a batch of biscuits. The cowboys had to eat and be out with the cattle at daybreak. As Cookie laid out a breakfast of coffee, biscuits, and beans, he called the cowboys once to come and get it. They either ate sitting on the ground or mounted their horses to eat in the saddle. The midday meal was a hurried one. Usually the cook baked up more sourdough biscuits, boiled some beans, fried steaks, or warmed up a stew from the previous night.

Supper, at the end of the day, was a bigger meal. Before digging into the chuck, the cowboys recited this ditty—

Thar's the bread, thar's the meat:
Now, by Joe, let's eat!

If whiskey was served with supper, they toasted each other with:

Up to my lips and over my gums—
Look out, guts, here she comes.

Beef was rarely eaten on the cattle drives because the herd was worth more at market than as food for the cowboys. But if a steer or a cow broke a leg during a stampede or a young calf was seriously injured on the trail,

then it was shot and butchered for meals. The meat was always cooked well-done because cowboys didn't care for it rare or semicooked. They also refused to eat raw vegetables and never touched mutton (lamb). They did love stew. One of their favorites was called "Son of a Gun Stew," consisting of a cow's heart, tongue, brains, liver, and marrow gut (a tube with marrow-like contents that connects the compartments of a cow's stomach).

Plenty of beans were served, too many at times, especially if a cattle owner was stingy with the food supplies for the trail ride. The cowboys gave the beans they ate on the trail nicknames like "prairie strawberries," "whistle beans," and "deceitful beans" because they talked behind your back. But the cowboys loved beans, especially pinto, named after the horse because of their spots. Beans and meat were seasoned with salt and pepper and sometimes an onion (called a "skunk egg" during cowboy times).

Cowboys in the late 1800s had no use for tea. Coffee, served strong and black, was drunk at every meal. If the cook watered it down too much, the cowboys called the weak brew "belly wash" or "brown gargle." Most trail hands refused to have their coffee sweetened or milky. They didn't like milking cows, so they learned to do without any kind of cream in their coffee. Even when canned milk became available, they still wouldn't have anything to do with the "canned cow." They feared their breath would smell like a young calf's.

A huge pot of coffee hung over the fire on an iron rod. If, during a meal, a cowboy got up to refill his cup and another trail-hand shouted, "Man at the pot," the cowboy had to go around and pour coffee in all the tin cups held out to him.

The Arbuckle brand of coffee was used so much on the trail that the cowboys didn't know of any other kind. Before the Civil War and right after, all coffee was shipped as green beans. People had to roast the beans in a skillet or an oven before grinding them. The Arbuckle Brothers, wholesale grocers from Pittsburgh, Pennsylvania, thought of a way to ship coffee beans already roasted: The Arbuckles coated the roasted beans with a mixture of sugar and egg whites to seal in the flavor and keep the beans fresh. These roasted beans were packed in bright yellow-and-red one-pound (45–kilogram) bags. The name ARBUCKLES' was printed in big letters across the front. Underneath the letters was a picture of a flying angel in a flowing gray skirt with a long red scarf around her neck. A stick of peppermint candy was packed inside each sack. If the cook was too busy to grind the beans, he'd call out for one of the cowboys to help him. Most of them rushed forward, because the one who ground the coffee got the candy.

Though much has been written about these large cattle drives, they didn't last forever. The trails eventually closed for several reasons. By the 1870s, the Homestead Act, passed in 1862, was starting to show its influ-

ence by the increased settlement of land on the open plains, dividing the trails with small ranches and farms. Then when barbed wire was invented in 1875, these settlers were able to build sturdy fences on their places, blocking the cattle trails even more. The weather also helped to put an end to the era of big cattle herds. A great drought in 1885 dried up the grass on the plains, and a hard winter in 1886 killed off entire herds. By the time Oklahoma was opened up to settlement in 1889, the cattle trails were closed for good.

And so the West was won by hardy men and women who left us a rich food history created along dusty trails and in muddy mining camps. When you make the recipes in this book, think of those pioneer cooks of long ago and give them a big cheer!

CHUCK WAGON BEANS

6–8 servings

You will need:
6 slices thick-cut bacon
1 small onion, diced
3 29-ounce cans of plain pinto beans
¼ cup brown sugar
1 cup dark molasses
2 tablespoons cider vinegar
2 teaspoons dry mustard
2 cloves garlic, minced

½ teaspoon cayenne
½ teaspoon chili powder

Equipment:
long fork
skillet
4-quart cooking pot
measuring cups and spoons
wooden spoon

What to do:
1. Using the long fork, fry bacon slices in skillet until soft and brown, but not crisp.
2. Add onion to bacon in skillet. Cook until onion turns clear.
3. Have an adult pour bacon and onions into cooking pot. Add beans, draining each can of beans first. Add remaining ingredients. Stir with wooden spoon.
4. Cover and simmer beans on low heat for about an hour.
5. Serve as a side dish or as the main part of a meal.

How Did the Cowboy Cook Make Chuck Wagon Beans?

Ingredients: Cookie used salt pork instead of bacon slices and dried pinto beans instead of canned beans because they were easier to carry on the chuck wagon. The day before cooking, the meal-handler had to pick through the beans and take out any rocks left purposely there by a farmer to make the beans weigh more at market. No cowboy wanted to break a tooth on a rock mixed in with his cooked beans. After sorting through the beans, Cookie washed them and set them to soak overnight. The next morning, he drained off the water, added new water, and put them on a slow fire to cook. As they cooked, Cookie added molasses, brown sugar, onions, and seasonings. Beans were never cooked less than five hours. They had to be tender, but not mushy.

Equipment: A Dutch oven was used to cook the beans over a fire. Another method was called "the bean hole." After the beans were washed and soaked, they were poured into a bucket with a tight lid that had been punctured a couple of times to let out steam. A hole was dug at the edge of the fire and the bucket was buried up to its lid. Hot ashes were placed around the lid to keep the beans simmering. Anyone, even a stranger stopping by the camp, would make sure hot coals surrounded the bucket. It was a courtesy of the land and the times.

APPENDIX

Additional directions for using recipes in a classroom with your teacher and 32 classmates:

Chapter 1
Bacon Cornbread: Equipment needed: portable toaster oven and one more baking pan. Increase ingredients: Double recipe and cut small squares.

Chapter 2
Skillet Bread: Equipment needed: portable toaster oven and two 10-inch pie pans instead of skillet.
Increase ingredients: Double recipe and cut into smaller wedges.
Dried Apple Pie: Equipment needed: portable toaster oven and one more 9-inch pie pan.
Increase ingredients: Double recipe and cut into small slices.

Chapter 3
Sourdough Starter: Equipment needed: one glass jar with lid and a dish towel for each classmate. Several wooden spoons to be shared.
Increase ingredients: Use a 10-pound sack of unbleached all-purpose flour, five pounds of sugar, and three quarts of buttermilk.
Sourdough Flapjacks: Equipment needed: electric griddle.
Increase ingredients: Double recipe and make each flapjack 2 inches wide instead of 4 inches.

Chapter 4
Cornish Pasties: Equipment needed: portable toaster oven.
Increase ingredients: Double recipe and cut into small pieces.

Chapter 5
Vinegar Pie: Equipment needed: portable toaster oven and one more 9-inch pie pan.
Increase ingredients: Double recipe and cut into small slices.

Chapter 6
Chuck Wagon Beans: Equipment needed: electric frying pan and one Crock-Pot™.
Increase ingredients: Double recipe. Allow for extra cooking time.

SOURCE NOTES

I gathered information for this project like ingredients for a recipe: a dash of this, a teaspoon of that, and sometimes whole cupfuls of colorful facts. *Wagon Wheel Kitchens: Food on the Oregon Trail* by Jacqueline Williams flavored Chapters 1 and 2 with a grand overview of the food supplies, cooking utensils, methods of meal preparation, and types of fuel used on the westward journey to Oregon in the mid-1800s. Numerous other books, including *Daily Life in a Covered Wagon* by Paul Erickson, *Beyond the Mississippi: Early Westward Expansion of the United States* by Angela M. Herb, and *Home on the Range: A Culinary History of the American West* by Cathy Luchetti, added the necessary grit by depicting the hardships of cooking in all kinds of weather over an unpredictable campfire. The historical facts in Chapter 3 came from a variety of gold rush books, but none was better at describing the everyday life of a forty-niner than the writings in *John Doble's Journal and Letters From the Mines*. In Chapter 4, I blended in facts about the foreigners, women, and African-Americans in the mining camps from books such as *They Saw the Elephant: Women in the California Gold Rush* by JoAnn Levy, *Hunter's Stew and Hangtown Fry: What Pioneer America Ate and Why* by Lila Perl, and *The Black West* by William Loren Katz. The cowboy era in Chapters 5 and 6 was the most fun to research. An amusing and peppery account of large cattle drives, the cowboys who led them, and Cookie, the cranky cowboy cook, appeared in *Come an' Get It: The Story of the Old Cowboy Cook* by Ramon F. Adams. Other texts were also full of information about cowboy customs, but *Come an' Get It* was the most detailed account.

Another excellent source was periodicals. *Cobblestone: The History Magazine for Young People* devoted its December 1981 issue to The Oregon Trail. *American Cowboy* magazine had an interesting article by Suzanne B. Bopp titled "Going Up the Trail." Also, several newspaper articles on the California gold rush era appearing in the *Modesto Bee* provided me with exciting accounts of the time.

I also visited museums and historical landmarks to bring all my research elements together. The Oregon Trail Interpretive Center in Baker City, Oregon, was breathtaking. The End of the Oregon Trail Interpretive Center in Oregon City presented a large supply of interesting pioneer stories, as did the Columbia Gorge Discovery Center Historical Museum in Wasco County, Oregon. The Fort Bridger Museum, Devil's Gate, Independence Rock, and Fort Laramie Museum allowed me to view what the pioneers had seen when passing through Wyoming on their way west. Lastly, the Columbia State Historic Park in California put on an enactment of an 1850s mining camp that entertained and enlightened me.

Loretta Ichord

BIBLIOGRAPHY

Adams, Ramon F. *Come an' Get It: The Story of the Old Cowboy Cook.* Norman: University of Oklahoma Press, 1952.

Bespalec, Kirsten, and Tamara Omtvedt, eds. *The Oregon Trail Cookbook.* Kearney, NE: Morris Publishing, 1993.

Bopp, Suzanne B. "Going Up the Trail: The Chisholm Trail Brought Longhorns to Kansas— and the Cowboy to the World." *American Cowboy*, May/June 2000, p. 74.

Doble, John. Charles L. Camp, ed. *John Doble's Journal and Letters From the Mines: Volcano, Mokelumne Hill, Jackson, and San Francisco, 1851–1865.* Volcano, CA: Volcano Press, 1999.

Dodge, Natt N. "Wild Life of the American West." In *The Book of the American West.* New York: Julian Messner, 1963.

Erickson, Paul. *Daily Life in a Covered Wagon.* New York: Puffin Books, 1997.

Gregory, Scott. *Sowbelly and Sourdough: Original Recipes from the Trail Drives and Cow Camps of the 1800s.* Caldwell, ID: Caxton Printers, 1995.

Herb, Angela M. *Beyond the Mississippi: Early Westward Expansion of the United States.* New York: Lodestar Books, 1996.

Katz, William Loren. *The Black West.* New York: Touchstone, 1996.

Leonard, Jonathan Norton, and the Editors of Time-Life Books. *American Cooking: The Great West.* New York: Time-Life Books, 1971.

Levy, JoAnn. *They Saw the Elephant: Women in the California Gold Rush.* Hamden, CT: Archon Books, 1990.

Luchetti, Cathy. *Home on the Range: A Culinary History of the American West.* New York: Villard Press, 1993.

Luchetti, Cathy, and Carol Olwell. *Women of the West.* New York: Crown Publishers, Inc., 1982.

Magagnini, Stephen. "Gold Was the Color That Mattered Most: Blacks Came Seeking Fortune—Many Found Freedom, Fame, Worthy Fights as Well." *Modesto Bee*, January 19, 1998.

Mooney, Michael G. "Cousin Jacks: Spirit of Cornish Miners Still Felt in Mother Lode." *Modesto Bee*, March 10, 1996.

Morley, Jacqueline. *How Would You Survive in the American West?* Danbury, CT: Franklin Watts, 1995.

Moulton, Candy. *Everyday Life in the Wild West From 1840–1900.* Cincinnati, OH: Writer's Digest Books, 1999.

"The Oregon Trail," *Cobblestone: The History Magazine for Young People,* December 1981.

Patent, Greg. *New Cooking from the Old West.* Berkeley, CA: Ten Speed Press, 1996.

Perl, Lila. *Hunter's Stew and Hangtown Fry: What Pioneer America Ate and Why.* New York: Seabury Press, 1977.

Schanzer, Rosalyn. *Gold Fever: Tales from the California Gold Rush.* Washington, D.C.: National Geographic Society, 1999.

Sherrow, Victoria. *Life During the Gold Rush.* San Diego, CA: Lucent Books, 1998.

Smith, Jeff. *The Frugal Gourmet Cooks American.* New York: William Morrow, 1987.

Steber, Rick. *Cowboys.* Volume 4 of Trails of the Wild West Series. Prineville, OR: Bonanza Publishing, 1988.

Walker, Barbara M. *The Little House Cookbook: Frontier Foods from Laura Ingalls Wilder's Classic Stories.* New York: Harper Trophy, 1979.

Wiegand, Steve. "An Era Remembered: Discovery Changes California Forever." *Modesto Bee,* January 18, 1998.

Williams, Jacqueline. *Wagon Wheel Kitchens: Food on the Oregon Trail.* Lawrence: University Press of Kansas, 1993.

INDEX

Abilene, Kansas, 46
African-Americans, 40–41, 46
Alcoholic drinks, 35
Apple pies, 22, 26–27, 58
Arbuckle coffee, 55

Bacon, 10
Bacon Cornbread, 15, 58
Bacteria, 13
Bait, 19
Baking powder, 25, 37
Baking soda, 11, 37
Barbed wire, 56
Beans, 54, 57
Beer (Hopper) Springs, 14
Blue Mountains, 23
Bread, 21–22, 34
    Bacon Cornbread, 15, 58
    Skillet Bread, 21, 24–25, 58
Bread-on-a-stick, 21
Brown sugar, 37
Buffalo, 17–20, 31
Buffalo birds, 19
Buffram, E. G., 33
Butter, 25, 51

Buttermilk, 25

California, 30, 31, 33–35, 38–41
Campfires, 17–19
Canned foods, 48
Cascade Mountains, 23
Cattle trails, 6, 45–56
Chinese miners, 38–39
Chisolm Trail, 46
Cholera, 13, 32
Chuck Wagon Beans, 57, 58
Chuck wagons, 46–49
Cinnamon sticks, 27
Coffee, 10, 34, 52, 54–55
Columbia River, 23
Cookie, 47–49
Cooking equipment, 11–12
Cornishmen, 39–40
Cornish Pasties, 42–43, 58
Cousin Jacks, 39, 43
Cowboys, 6, 45–56

Dennis, George Washington, 41

Devil's Gate, Wyoming, 23
Diseases
    cholera, 13, 32
    dysentery, 13, 32
    malaria, 32
    scurvy, 33
Doble, John, 33
Dried Apple Pie, 26–27, 58
Drycamping, 12, 17
Dry Diggins, California, 34
Ducks, 19
Dutch ovens, 11, 25, 27, 43, 57
Dysentery, 13, 32

Eggs, 9, 34, 37, 51

Fishing, 19, 34
Flapjacks, 35, 37
Flour, 25, 34
Food supplies, 10–11
Fort Kearny, 17
Fort Laramie, 22, 31
Forty-niners, 6, 30–43
Fourth of July, 22, 23
Fruits, 21, 22

Giant Register of the Desert, 22
Gold miners, 6, 30–43
Great American Desert, 16
Great Plains, 16, 17, 31

Hangtown, California, 34–35
Hangtown Fry, 35
Hardtack, 12, 31, 33
Homestead Act of 1862, 55–56
Hunting, 19, 20, 34

Ice Springs Slough, Wyoming, 13–14
Idaho, 8, 13, 14, 25
Independence, Missouri, 5
Independence Rock, Wyoming, 22, 23
Isthmus of Panama, 32

Jackrabbits, 19
Jerky, 20, 33

Lettuce, 33
Lucifers, 18

Malaria, 32
Marshall, James, 30
Matches, 18–19
Milk, 37, 40, 54
Miner's lettuce, 33
Missouri River, 12
Molasses, 31
Mosquitoes, 32
Mother Lode, 33

Native Americans, 9, 20–21, 31, 34, 46
Nooning, 17

North Platte River, 12

Oklahoma, 56
Onions, 54
Oregon Trail, 5, 6, 9, 12, 23, 31
Ovens
    Dutch, 11, 25, 27, 43, 57
    reflector, 11, 27

Pancakes, 35
Pasties, 39–40, 42
Phelps, Mrs., 40
Pioneers, 5–27
Placerville, California, 35, 40
Plains Indians, 31
Plants, 21, 22
Platte River, 12
Possibles drawer, 49
Possum belly, 49
Prairie chickens (grouse), 19
Prairie dogs, 19
Pronghorn antelope, 19

Recipes
    Bacon Cornbread, 15, 58
    Chuck Wagon Beans, 57, 58
    Cornish Pasties, 42–43, 58
    Dried Apple Pie, 26–27, 58
    Skillet Bread, 24–25, 58
    Sourdough Flapjacks, 37, 58
    Sourdough Starter, 36, 58
    Vinegar Pie, 50–51, 58
Reflector ovens, 11, 27
Rocky Mountains, 8, 18, 23, 31

Sagebrush, 18
Saleratus, 11, 22, 25, 37

Scurvy, 33
Sea voyages, 31–32
Sierra Mountains, 30, 33
Skillet Bread, 21, 24–25, 58
Snake River, 12
Soda Springs, Idaho, 14
Son of a Gun Stew, 54
Sourdough biscuits, 49, 52
Sourdough Flapjacks, 37, 58
Sourdough keg, 48, 49
Sourdough Starter, 35, 36, 58
South Pass, 23
Spotted Pup, 49
Starters, 22
Starvation, 31
Sugar, 27, 37
Sutter's Mill, 30
Sweetwater Mountain Ice Cream, 23
Sweetwater River, 12, 14, 23, 25

Tent cities, 33
Texas, 46
Tommyknockers, 40
Trout, 19

Vinegar, 12–13, 31
Vinegar Pie, 50–51, 58
Vitamin C, 33

Wakefield, Lucy Stoddard, 40
Washington State, 8
Water, 12–14
Water kegs, 12
Wild yeast, 21, 22, 36
Willamette Valley, 23
Wyoming, 13, 22, 25

Yeast breads, 21–22

64